FAR-OUT GUIDE TO THE

MOON

Mary Kay Carson

Bailey Books
an imprint of
Enslow Publishers, Inc.
40 Industrial Road
Box 398
Berkeley Heights, NJ 07922
USA
http://www.enslow.com

For Kylie Anah Hammons

Bailey Books, an imprint of Enslow Publishers, Inc.

Library of Congress Cataloging-in-Publication Data

Carson, Mary Kay.
    Far-out guide to the moon / Mary Kay Carson.
        p. cm. — (Far-out guide to the solar system)
    Summary: "Presents information about the moon, including fast facts, history, and technology used to
study it"—Provided by publisher.
    Includes bibliographical references and index.
    ISBN 978-0-7660-3189-0 (Library Ed.)
    ISBN 978-1-59845-184-9 (Paperback Ed.)
    1. Moon—Juvenile literature. 2. Solar system—Juvenile literature. I. Title.
    QB582.C38 2011
    523.3—dc22

                2009006487

Paperback ISBN 978-1-59845-184-9

Image Credits: AOES Medialab, ESA 2002, p. 19; Apollo 17/NASA, p. 11; Copyright António Cidadão, p. 24; ESA
- AOES Medialab, p. 42; ESA/Space-X (Space Exploration Institute), p. 28; Illustration by AOES Medialab, ESA
2002, p. 4; Lockheed Martin Corp., pp. 27, 41; Lunar and Planetary Institute, p. 13; NASA Johnson Space Center
(NASA-JSC), p. 17; NASA, pp. 1, 9, 15, 22, 34; NASA/JPL, pp. 3, 36–37; NASA/JPL/USGS, pp. 12, 30; NASA/Regan
Geeseman, p. 39; National Space Science Data Center, NASA Goddard Space Flight Center, p. 8; Russ Underwood,
Lockheed Martin Missiles & Space, p. 32; Southwest Research Institute, p. 18; Tom Uhlman, pp. 7, 21; William
Feldman/Los Alamos National Labs, p. 33.

Cover Image: NASA

CONTENTS

Moon

EARTH'S moon is a giant.
The Earth and Moon are closer
in size than any other moon-and-
planet pair in the solar system.

INTRODUCTION

★

Did you know that the Moon is moving away from us? Every year the Moon moves nearly 4 centimeters (1½ inches) farther away from Earth. How do we know this? Scientists measure the distance between Earth and the Moon using mirrors put on the Moon by astronauts. You will learn many more far-out facts about the Moon in this book. Just keep reading!

The Moon is Earth's only natural satellite. A satellite travels around, or orbits, another space object. Many artificial satellites orbit Earth, sending down TV signals and other information. But only one natural satellite, or moon, circles our planet. Because it is Earth's only moon, we call it *the* Moon. The Moon is unique in the solar system, too. It is the largest moon compared to its planet. While some of Jupiter's and one of Saturn's moons are bigger, all are tiny compared to their giant planets. The Moon's width is about one-quarter of Earth's width. That is

A FAMILIAR FACE

The Moon's shape in the night sky looks as if it changes during the month. These different moon shapes are called phases. Earth goes around the Sun. The Moon orbits Earth. The changing positions of these three objects create the lunar phases. When the Moon is between Earth and the Sun, the shadowed side of the Moon faces us. This is a dark New Moon. When Earth is between the Sun and the Moon, the completely sunlit side faces us. This is a Full Moon. First quarter, third quarter, and other phases are steps along the way from New Moon to Full Moon and back again.

BOTH FAMILIAR AND MYSTERIOUS

The Moon is an ordinary sight, as well as its own extraordinary world. Humans have studied the Moon for a long time. Ancient people used the changing Moon phases as a calendar. Modern people have peered at the Moon through telescopes and realized it was a world beyond Earth. During the space age, people sent rockets and astronauts to explore our closest neighbor in space.

Twelve astronauts have walked on the Moon. It is the only other world visited by humans. Over the years, more than seventy-five spacecraft have flown by, circled, or landed on the Moon. More robotic spacecraft, or space probes, will be joining them soon. The 2010s are the International Lunar Decade. Moon missions from China, India, Japan, Europe, and the United States are planned.

The Moon has been visited and well mapped. But much is still mysterious about it. Scientists still wonder: What lies underneath its crater-covered crust? What causes

WHAT do you think about when you look at the Moon? Is it a pretty sight, a marker of time, a world to explore, or something else?

FAR-OUT FACT

LOVELY LUNA

We call our only moon *the* Moon, but many call it by its Latin name—Luna. The word to describe moon things—*lunar*—comes from this name. There are lunar spacecraft, lunar astronauts, lunar rocks, lunar space suits, lunar rovers, and more.

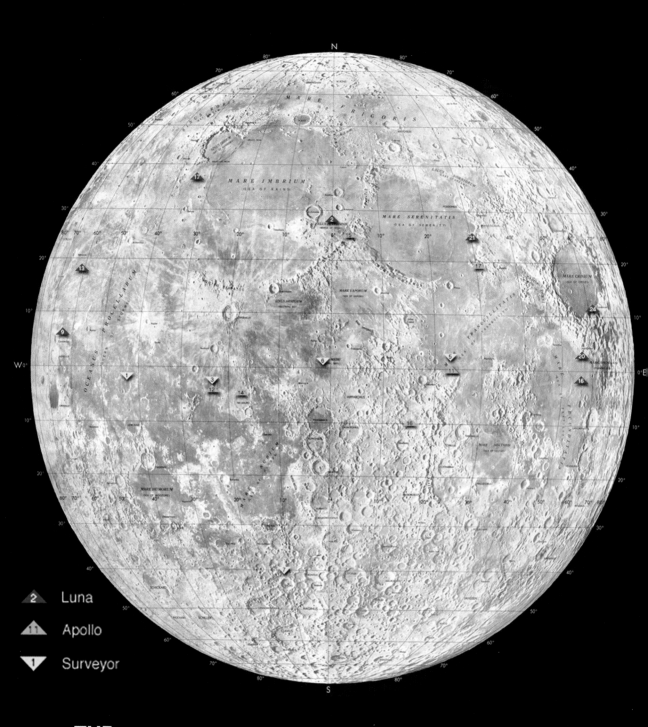

2 Luna

11 Apollo

1 Surveyor

THE triangles on this map of the Moon mark the many places where lunar spacecraft have landed. The red triangles are where robotic Russian landers set down from 1959 to 1976. The yellow triangles are where robotic American landers touched down from 1966 to 1968. The six green triangles are where the U.S. astronaut missions landed in 1969 to 1972.

ONLY four of our solar system's moons are bigger than Earth's moon: Ganymede, Callisto, and Io of Jupiter; and Saturn's Titan.

moonquakes? How much water ice is on the Moon? We want to know more about our moon, because its history is our history. The Moon affects Earth every day. We will share a changing future, too. Someday, humans may even live on the Moon.

CHAPTER I

WHERE DID THE MOON COME FROM?

Astronaut Buzz Aldrin stepped out onto the Moon in 1969. He took a long look around. Then he declared that he saw "a magnificent desolation." What did the astronaut mean? The Moon is a still, empty, lonely—or desolate—world. Not a single weed or bug lives there. The lunar landscape looks like a black-and-white movie. Nearly every pebble, rock, and boulder is a shade of gray. The daytime sky is inky black. There is no air on the Moon. No breeze blows the dust blanketing its bare ground.

The Moon is also a magnificent sight, as Aldrin said. Millions of craters cover its surface. Space rocks slamming into the Moon created these bowl-shaped dents.

APOLLO 17 astronaut Harrison Schmitt uses the lunar rover to explore the lifeless, still, gray Moon in 1972.

FAR-OUT FACT

GIANT STEPS FOR MANKIND

Apollo was **NASA's** program to send astronauts to the Moon. In 1969, *Apollo 11* delivered the first humans to the Moon's surface, Neil Armstrong and Buzz Aldrin. *Apollo 12, 14, 15, 16,* and *17* also landed two astronauts each on the Moon, while a third astronaut remained in the orbiting spacecraft. (*Apollo 13* did not make it to the Moon.) While there, the twelve Apollo moon astronauts studied the solar wind, Moon rocks and soil, meteoroids, temperature, magnetic fields, and moonquakes.

Meteoroids, asteroids, and comets have left craters of all sizes on the Moon. They range from tiny dimples in the dust to holes bigger than Texas. Some recent craters are surrounded by streaky rays. The rays are bright material splashed out at impact. The largest moon craters are ringed in rims as tall as mountains. Highlands like these look light-colored from Earth. The areas of the Moon that look dark from Earth are called maria (seas). The dark maria were once oceans of lava. They cooled into flat plains of rock billions of years ago.

THIS is the near side of the Moon, the side always turned toward Earth. You can see the dark maria, the lighter highlands, and the bright rays surrounding the 85-kilometer- (52-mile-) wide Tycho crater near the bottom.

ON this color-coded map of the Moon, red shows high areas and purple shows low areas. Which areas have the most craters, highlands or lowland maria?

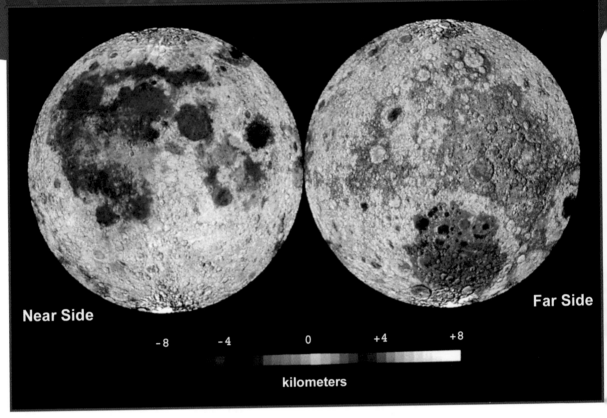

Near Side

Far Side

-8 -4 0 +4 +8

kilometers

ROCKY CLUES AND BIG QUESTIONS

The Apollo astronaut missions taught us a lot about the Moon. The more than 2,000 Moon rocks they brought back have given scientists a lot of clues about how the Moon and Earth are alike—and different. Most of the Moon's surface is older than Earth's surface. The youngest Moon rocks are nearly as old as the oldest rocks on Earth. Ancient Moon rocks are still around because the Moon's surface is not constantly changing like Earth's. There is no liquid water or wind on the Moon to break rocks down. No volcanoes have spewed lava and made new rocks on the Moon for more than a million years.

Earth and the Moon are made up of the same ingredients, just in different amounts. It is like cookies compared to cake—same stuff but in different amounts. Earth is heavier and denser than the Moon and has more iron. Nearly all Earth rocks have some water in them, too, unlike Moon rocks. "[L]unar rocks are extremely parched," says Robin Canup. Canup is an expert on how planets and moons form. The scientist works on one mystery the Apollo mission could not solve: Where did the Moon come from?

Scientists have long wondered about this question. Did the Moon form alongside Earth out of the same cloud of dust and gas as Earth and the rest of the planets? Was the Moon instead born elsewhere and then later captured into Earth's orbit? Or perhaps while the Earth was young and still mostly melted rock, a mushy blob of it broke off and became the Moon.

All of these ideas, or theories, have problems. The Moon is too similar to Earth to have formed somewhere else and then been captured. But the Moon is also too different to have formed alongside Earth or be a broken-off chunk. A decade after the Apollo missions ended, scientists accepted a different idea for how the Moon formed. It is called the Giant Impact Theory.

IN 1969, astronaut Buzz Aldrin set up an instrument to measure moonquakes.

MOONQUAKES

When the ground beneath you moves and shakes, it is an earthquake. On the Moon, it is called a moonquake. Scientists are not sure what causes moonquakes. Apollo astronauts set up moonquake-measuring instruments called seismometers. They showed the Moon to be a mysteriously moving place! Most moonquakes are weak. But in only five years, the Apollo-installed seismometers measured 28 powerful, long-lasting moonquakes. Some were strong enough to damage a future Moon base, so engineers will need to design quake-proof Moon buildings.

THE BIG WHACK

"The basic idea is that about 4.5 billion years ago Earth collided with an object roughly the size of the current planet Mars," explains Robin Canup. "And this collision was so massive that it launched material into orbit around the Earth." The circling material later clumped and lumped into a big ball—the Moon. Canup uses a computer program to test the theory. It divides the young Earth and the impacting object into 120,000 particles.

THE 2,415 Moon rocks vary from sand-like grains to basketball-sized stones. Astronauts chipped the Moon rock below off a large boulder in a highlands area. A scientist (at right) in 1971 uses a microscope to get an up-close look at a Moon rock.

These show up as dots on a computer screen. Then the program tracks each particle as the two worlds collide, slosh together, and reshape into two separate spheres.

Canup's computer program helps explain why Earth has more iron and water than the Moon. Most of the heavy iron inside the impacting object mixes in with a reshaping Earth. It is left out of the less heavy Moon. And the new Moon's surface was an ocean of hot lava for a long while. This baked away the Moon's water. Studying how the Moon formed also teaches us a lot about Earth.

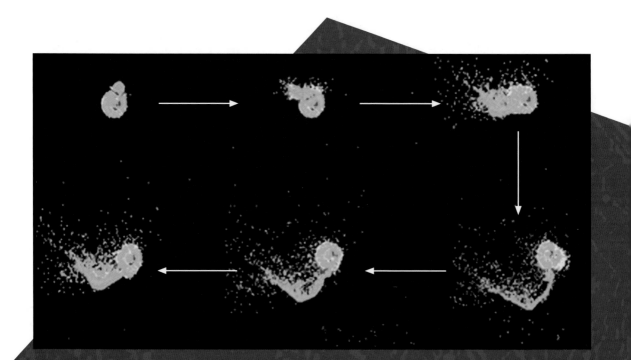

THIS computer program shows what could have happened step by step if a Mars-sized object had hit a young Earth.

THIS illustration shows a Mars-sized object slamming into Earth 4.5 billion years ago. Scientists think the material thrown into Earth orbit from the impact eventually became the Moon.

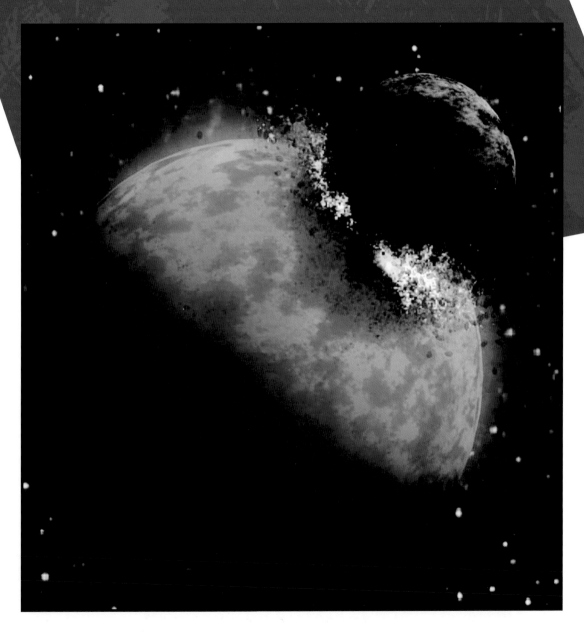

A Mars-sized object slamming into a young Earth likely changed its spin. "It's what gave us our current 24-hour day, we believe," says Canup.

The Moon also affects Earth's climate. Its gravity keeps Earth from wobbling. "If we didn't have the Moon, or if we had a much smaller moon . . . the tilt of our north pole would vary widely," explains Canup. Earth's tilt is what creates our seasons. A wobbling Earth would make it harder for life to survive. It would be a world where the seasons suddenly switch. The weather would constantly change. The Moon makes Earth an easier place to live.

FAR-OUT FACT

WATERY TUG-OF-WAR

The Moon's tugging gravity is what makes ocean waters rise and fall—the tides. The side of Earth nearest the Moon gets the strongest pull, so this is where high tide happens. On the opposite side of Earth, the Moon's pull is weakest, so the water sags away from the Moon, creating another high tide. In between these two bulging sides is where low tides are. Every beach has two high and two low tides every day as Earth spins around once. Tides shape coastlines, mix ocean waters, and create shoreline habitats.

TIDAL pools and tidal zones are flooded at high tide, but are left exposed at low tide. Unique kinds of plants and animals—including barnacles, seaweed, starfish, crabs, and shorebirds—live in these tidal habitats.

Moon at a Glance

Diameter: 3,475 kilometers (2,159 miles)

Volume: 2 percent of Earth's

Mass: 1.2 percent of Earth's, or
73,483,000,000,000,000,000,000 kilograms

Gravity: 1/6 of Earth's; a 75-pound kid would
weigh 12½ pounds

Average Distance from Earth: 384,400 kilometers
(238,855 miles)

Day Length: 655 hours, 43 minutes

Year Length: 27.3 Earth days to orbit Earth once

Color: Gray

Atmosphere: None

Surface: Rocky and dusty

Lowest/Highest Surface Temperatures: −233/123° Celsius
(−387/253° Fahrenheit)

Namesake: Luna was Roman moon goddess

Symbol:

Moon Fast Facts

★ The Moon is Earth's only natural satellite.

★ Earth's moon is the fifth largest moon in the solar system.

★ The Moon is the largest natural satellite compared to its planet, Earth.

★ The Moon has no air, clouds, or weather, and no life.

★ The Moon gets both very cold and very hot. When the Sun is shining, temperatures soar to 123°C (253°F). Then it can drop to –233°C (–387°F) at night.

★ The Moon's gravity is about 1/6 of Earth's, and is why astronauts can jump so high on the Moon.

★ Gray powdery soil called lunar regolith covers the Moon's surface.

★ We always see the same side of the Moon, called the near side. The Moon spins once during each Earth orbit, causing the same side to always face Earth.

★ The lighter-colored areas of the Moon are called highlands. The dark areas are ancient lava plains called maria.

★ Maria cover about 16 percent of the Moon, and highlands 84 percent. However, the near side that we always see is about 30 percent maria.

★ Earth's ocean tides are caused by the Moon's gravitational pull. High tides happen on the side of the Earth that is facing the Moon, and also on the opposite side.

★ Scientists think that a Mars-sized object slammed into Earth about 4.5 billion years ago, throwing material into orbit around Earth that later clumped into the Moon.

23

★ The Moon's surface does not change much over time. There are no active volcanoes, no wind, and no rain.

★ Moonquakes are vibrations beneath the Moon's surface. No one is sure what causes them.

★ If you were on the Moon looking at Earth, our planet would look four times bigger than a Full Moon.

★ During a lunar eclipse, Earth blocks the sunlight that normally shines on the Moon. From Earth, it looks as if the Moon gets dark.

★ The Moon's shape seems to change. Theses shapes, or phases, are created by the regularly changing positions of the Sun, Moon, and Earth. We only see the part of the Moon that is lit up by the Sun as the Moon orbits Earth.

THE Moon's appearance changes over one month. It starts as a dark New Moon. Then it becomes a small crescent (top left), a quarter Moon (second row), and then a Full Moon (fourth row, left). Over the next two weeks, it slowly returns to a dark New Moon again (bottom right).

Crater Fast Facts

★ The Moon's surface is covered in impact craters from meteoroids, comets, and asteroids that have struck it over billions of years.

★ The Moon's millions of craters range in size from microscopic to 2,100 kilometers (1,300 miles) wide and 4,500 meters (15,000 feet) deep.

★ Some of the deepest craters cast permanent shadows, creating always-dark areas where ice survives.

★ Tycho crater is more than 85 kilometers (52 miles) wide and 100 million years old.

Mission Fast Facts

★ More than seventy-five spacecraft have gone to the Moon.

★ The space probe *Luna 3*'s photographs gave us the first view of the Moon's far side in 1959.

★ On July 20, 1969, Neil Armstrong became the first human being to set foot on the Moon.

★ Between 1969 and 1972, twelve astronauts from NASA's Apollo program walked on the Moon.

★ Apollo astronauts brought back 382 kilograms (842 pounds) of lunar rocks and soil.

★ It only takes about seventy hours to get to the Moon by spacecraft.

★ A spacecraft called *LCROSS (Lunar Crater Observation and Sensing Satellite)* purposely crashes into crater Cabeus near the Moon's south pole and discovers water.

★ NASA plans to send astronauts back to the Moon by 2020, nearly a half century after the last person walked on the Moon in 1972.

Moon

Timeline of Exploration and Discovery

PREHISTORY—Humans mark the passage of time with lunar phases and moonrises.

1609—Galileo sees the Moon's craters and mountains with his telescope.

1651—Giovanni Battista Riccioli and Francesco M. Grimaldi complete a map of the Moon.

1840—First close-up photographs of the Moon are taken through a telescope.

1892—Grove Karl Gilbert argues that most lunar craters are impact craters, not volcanic craters.

1959—*Luna 1* probe makes the first lunar flyby in January. *Luna 2* and *3* follow that fall.

1964—*Ranger 7* space probe sends back the first close-up photographs of the Moon.

1966—*Luna 9* space probe makes the first soft lunar landing.

1966–1967—Five Lunar Orbiter spacecraft make a photographic map of the Moon.

1968—*Apollo 8* becomes first piloted flight to the Moon, circling it ten times before returning to Earth.

1969—*Apollo 11*, first human landing on the Moon, returns with rock and soil samples. *Apollo 12* lands astronauts on the Ocean of Storms area.

1970—*Apollo 13* fails to reach the Moon, but astronauts safely return to Earth.

1971—*Apollo 14* lands astronauts in the Moon's Fra Mauro highlands. *Apollo 15* lands astronauts in the Moon's Hadley Rille-Apennine area.

1970-1976—Robotic spacecraft *Luna 16*, *Luna 20*, and *Luna 24* return a total of 300 grams (10½ ounces) of lunar soil samples to Earth.

1972—*Apollo 16* lands astronauts in Descartes crater. *Apollo 17* is the final of six successful missions to land astronauts and return samples from the Moon. Astronaut Harrison Schmitt becomes the first scientist to visit the Moon.

1975—William K. Hartmann and Donald R. Davis suggest the Moon formed through the Giant Impact Theory.

1994—*Clementine* orbiter creates the first topographic lunar map and finds possible evidence of water ice.

1998—*Lunar Prospector* searches for ice at the Moon's poles and maps lunar resources, gravity, and magnetic fields. It finds no definite evidence of water.

2004—European orbiter *SMART-1* orbits and maps the Moon.

2007—Japan's *Kaguya* orbiter team begins mapping the Moon's surface in high definition. China's *Chang'e 1* orbiter maps the Moon and measures lunar soil depth.

2008—India's *Chandrayaan-1* orbiter begins mapping the Moon's minerals and finds evidence of water a year later.

2009—*Lunar Reconnaissance Orbiter (LRO)* searches for future astronaut landing sites. *Lunar Crater Observation and Sensing Satellite (LCROSS)* impacts the Moon's south pole, finding water in the plume of kicked-up debris.

2010—China's *Chang'e 2* lunar orbiter is scheduled to launch.

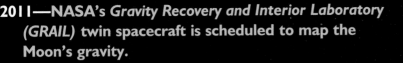

2011—NASA's *Gravity Recovery and Interior Laboratory (GRAIL)* twin spacecraft is scheduled to map the Moon's gravity.

2012—Russia's *Luna Glob* orbiter is scheduled to set up a seismic network on the Moon. *Lunar Atmosphere and Dust Environment Explorer (LADEE)* is scheduled to study the Moon's atmosphere from lunar orbit.

2020—NASA's Constellation program is scheduled to send four astronauts to the Moon aboard *Orion*.

SHACKLETON moon crater
was named for Ernest Shackleton.
He was a famous Antarctic explorer.
This 19-kilometer- (12-mile-) wide dark
crater lies near the lunar South Pole.
Sunlight never reaches into parts of
some of these shadowed steep craters.

CHAPTER 2

LOOKING FOR LUNAR ICE

Lunar rocks lost their water long ago. So the Moon is a totally dry world, right? Not necessarily. Remember that the Moon is covered in impact craters. Many of those impacting comets, asteroids, and meteoroids delivered some water ice to the Moon. The ice carried by space rocks scattered across the lunar surface upon impact. Sunlight quickly evaporated most of the ice. But scientists suspect that some of that water ice still survives on the Moon.

"The only way water can be preserved on the Moon . . . is in extremely cold areas," explains lunar scientist Alan Binder. The coldest places on the Moon are where the Sun never shines. Some of the Moon's

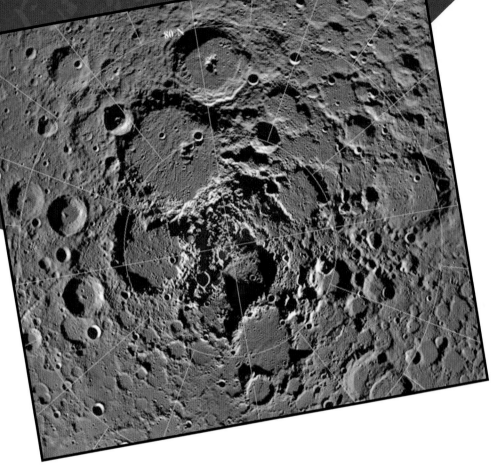

deep craters cast permanent shadows. The Moon's north and south poles have some always-dark craters. How much ice survives in these "cold trap" craters? Scientists are working to find out. Finding a lot of ice on the Moon would be a big deal. If humans are going to build a moon base someday, they will need water. Not having to bring water from Earth would be a big help.

SEARCHING THE SHADOWS

Two decades passed without a single lunar visitor after the last astronaut walked on the Moon in 1972. Another spacecraft finally headed to our orbiting neighbor in 1994. No humans were aboard *Clementine* when it launched. It was a robotic space probe. *Clementine* mapped the Moon's surface. It found permanently dark craters near the Moon's poles. *Clementine*'s radar also found hints of ice in those craters. But when radar telescopes on Earth looked, they could not find the lunar ice. So was it really there?

Lunar Prospector went to find out in 1998. The small space probe scanned the Moon's surface. Seven weeks after orbiting, *Lunar Prospector* scientists made a big announcement. "We have found water at both lunar poles," Alan Binder told reporters in March of 1998. He was in charge of the Lunar Prospector mission. Water ice crystals seemed to be mixed in with the dusty lunar soil. Lunar Prospector scientists said that a small lake's worth of water lay scattered as frost near the Moon's poles.

How could scientists be sure this time? They sacrificed their spacecraft to find out. In July of 1999, engineers

AN engineer gets *Lunar Prospector* ready for its 1998 launch. The small robotic space probe weighed less than a car.

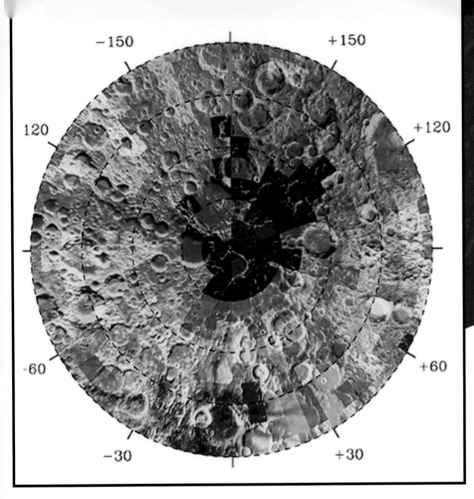

north pole. It shows hydrogen that's likely from water ice. Purple and blue areas have the most hydrogen. Green areas have a little hydrogen, and orange and yellow areas have the least. Where is the most hydrogen?

sent *Lunar Prospector* crashing into a dark crater at the Moon's south pole. Scientists figured that the crash's dust cloud would have some water vapor in it. But no water showed up. The mystery of water on the Moon would take another ten years to solve.

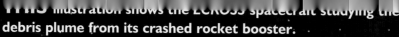
This illustration shows the LCROSS spacecraft studying the debris plume from its crashed rocket booster.

MORE THAN EXPECTED

When the robotic explorer *Lunar Reconnaissance Orbiter* flew to the Moon in 2009, another spacecraft piggybacked on it. The *Lunar Crater Observation and Sensing Satellite (LCROSS)* aimed to finally answer whether or not there is ice on the Moon. Soon after launch, *LCROSS* separated from its ride and headed for crater Cabeus near the Moon's south pole. First *LCROSS* sent its booster rocket crashing into the crater. The spacecraft quickly radioed back what it saw in the debris cloud. Only minutes later *LCROSS* slammed itself into the crater, too, as astronomers on Earth searched the kicked-up cloud for water—and found it.

"Yes, we found water," *LCROSS* scientist Anthony Colaprete told reporters during the big announcement in late 2009. "And we didn't find just a little bit." They'd found enough water to fill a dozen two-gallon buckets. There's likely a lot of ice on the Moon.

While *LCROSS* solved the Moon's water mystery, it created another one. Scientist haven't been able to identify some of the materials kicked-up into the debris cloud—yet. Scientists hope to find out what else might be hiding in them.

WHAT'S NEXT FOR THE MOON?

The Moon is a busy place these days. And it is getting busier! By 2012, a half dozen or more robotic spacecraft could be circling the Moon. (Check out the Moon Timeline of Exploration and Discovery on page 27.) These lunar orbiters come from many different places—Japan, China, Europe, India, and the United States. Some are already hard at work. Moon orbiter *Kaguya* has been making 3-D maps and high definition videos of the Moon's surface since 2007. The *Lunar Reconnaissance Orbiter* started looking for water ice and minerals on the Moon in 2009. It can see things as small as a 61-centimeter-

THIS illustration shows the twin robotic spacecraft called *GRAIL* measuring and mapping the Moon's uneven gravity.

BUMPY GRAVITY

Gravity on the Moon is not even. An astronaut weighs more while standing in an ancient lunar lava sea than elsewhere on the Moon. Why? Denser materials buried under the maria create more gravitational pull. Luckily robotic orbiters in the 1960s discovered the irregular "bumps" of gravity before astronauts tried to land on the Moon. The gravity bumps can send spacecraft nose-diving into Moon dust.

Future space probes will get a look beneath the Moon's gray dusty surface. *Gravity Recovery and Interior Laboratory* (*GRAIL*) is a twin space probe mission. *GRAIL* is set to launch in 2011. The space probe pair will fly around the Moon measuring and mapping its uneven gravity. *GRAIL* will also give scientists a peek inside the Moon all the way to its core.

These robotic explorers will teach us a lot about our nearby neighbor. Many of the maps these lunar probes are making will be used in the next step of lunar exploration. They will help send humans back to the Moon.

ENGINEERS field test NASA's new design for a Lunar Electric Rover by driving it over rough lava in the desert. Two astronauts will be able to live in the rover for up to 14 days and the vehicle can travel for thousands of miles.

ASTRONAUT, COSMONAUT, OR TAIKONAUT?

When **NASA** started its human spaceflight program in the late 1950s, it called the men in shiny suits astronauts. Astro means "star" and naut means "sailor," so astronauts are "star sailors." The Soviet Union (now Russia) called its space-traveling pioneers cosmonauts, which means "universe sailors." Cosmonaut Yuri Gagarin became the first man in space in 1961. Space travelers in China's space agency are called taikonauts, or "space sailors." In 2003, Yang Liwei became the first taikonaut.

GOING BACK TO STAY

No person has walked on the Moon in nearly four decades. The last lunar astronauts returned to Earth in 1972. Is it time for humans to go back to the Moon? NASA thinks so. Its Constellation program plans to send a four-person crew to the Moon by 2020. Unlike the Apollo missions, the Constellation program aims to send humans to the Moon to stay. It is part of a long-term plan to build a moon base and eventually send astronauts to Mars.

NASA astronauts will not likely be alone on the Moon. Other space agencies are also planning crewed Moon missions. The European Space Agency's (ESA's) Aurora Programme plans to land people on the Moon, too. Russian cosmonauts and Chinese taikonauts may also soon hop and walk on the Moon. Flying astronauts to

THIS illustration shows *Orion* arriving at the Moon. *Orion* is an astronaut-carrying spacecraft, or crew capsule, that **NASA** is building. *Orion* will begin flying astronauts to the *International Space Station* in 2015, and then to the Moon around 2020.

WHAT do you think a moon base might look like? This illustration shows one idea. Once a moon base is up and running, tourists may start visiting. After all, the Moon is very close. It takes less time to fly to the Moon than to travel across the United States by car.

the Moon and building a moon base will be difficult and expensive. Countries will likely cooperate, as they did when building the *International Space Station* that currently orbits Earth. Sharing technology and information and cooperating on Moon missions is what the International Lunar Decade is all about. It is also a celebration of our very special Moon, and its magnificent desolation.

FAR-OUT FACT

A VIEW FROM THE MOON

Why build a moon base? Many say it is the best way to learn how to live in space. They argue that humans cannot travel to other planets, like Mars, until they know how to live safely in space. The Moon is a nearby place to practice space life. Another benefit could be clearer telescope images. The Moon has no blurring air or fuzzy clouds. Telescopes on the Moon would have a clearer view of distant stars. A lunar observatory might even help find planets around other suns.

Words to Know

asteroid—A large rock, smaller than a planet or dwarf planet, that orbits the Sun.

atmosphere—The gases that are held by gravity around a planet, moon, or other object in space.

comet—A large chunk of frozen gases, ice, and dust that orbits the Sun.

craters—Bowl-shaped holes made by impact explosions on the surface of a planet or moon, often from comet or asteroid crashes.

diameter—A straight line through the center of a sphere or circle.

gravity—An attractive force on one object from another.

lander—A space probe that sets down on the surface of a planet or other object in space.

lava—Melted rock that comes out of a volcano.

lunar—Moon related.

magnetic field—The area of magnetic influence around a magnet, electric current, or planet.

maria—Dark, flat, lowland plain areas on the Moon. One of them is called a mare.

mass—The amount of matter in something.

meteoroid—A small chunk of space rock, often from crushed asteroids or broken-up comets.

moon—An object in space that naturally orbits a larger object in space.

NASA—The National Aeronautics and Space Administration, the space agency of the United States.

natural satellite—A moon.

orbit—The path followed by a planet, moon, or other object in space around another object in space.

orbiter—A space probe that orbits a planet, moon, or other object in space.

planet—A large, sphere-shaped object in space that is alone (except for its moons) in its orbit around a sun.

pole—One of two points on a sphere farthest from the equator; or either end of a magnet.

radar—A technology or device that uses reflected radio waves to find or map distant or unseen objects.

ray—Bright streaks around a moon crater.

regolith—Rocks, soil, and dust on the surface of the Moon.

rover—A mobile robot or vehicle that explores the surface of a planet or other object in space.

satellite—An object that orbits a larger object, such as a moon or a machine launched into space that orbits Earth.

space probe—A robotic spacecraft launched into space to collect information.

tides—The rise and fall of Earth's oceans.

year—The time it takes for an object in space to travel once around the Sun.

Find Out More and Get Updates

BOOKS

Bourgeois, Paulette. *The Jumbo Book of Space*. Toronto: Kids Can Press, 2007.

Carson, Mary Kay. *Exploring the Solar System: A History with 22 Activities*. Chicago: Chicago Review Press, 2008.

Fraknoi, Andrew. *Wonderful World of Space*. New York: Disney Publishing, 2007.

Thimmesh, Catherine. *Team Moon: How 400,000 People Landed Apollo 11 on the Moon*. Boston: Houghton Mifflin, 2006.

FIND OUT MORE AND GET UPDATES
★

MOON EXPLORATIONS WEB SITES

Interactive Lunar Exploration Timeline.
  http://www.lpi.usra.edu/lunar/missions

Lunar Reconnaissance Orbiter for Kids.
  http://lunar.gsfc.nasa.gov/forkids.html

MOON MISSION MOVIES

  http://www.nasa.gov/mission_pages/constellation/multimedia/

  (Browse the Video Gallery to see movies about the *Constellation*
  program, the Ares rocket, and the *Orion* crew capsule.)

MOON WATCHING WEB SITES

NightSky Sky Calendar.
  http://www.space.com/spacewatch/sky_calendar.html

StarDate Online.
  Nightsky Almanac: http://stardate.org/nightsky/almanac/

SOLAR SYSTEM WEB SITES

Solar System Exploration.
  http://solarsystem.nasa.gov/kids

Windows to the Universe.
  http://www.windows.ucar.edu/tour/link=/earth/moons_
  and_rings.html

Index